BORROWED IMAGES

Prose Poems

PIERCE TAYLOR HIBBS

Paperback ISBN: 979-8-9861067-3-1

Other Books by the Author

In Divine Company
Theological English
The Trinity, Language, and Human Behavior
The Speaking Trinity & His Worded World
Finding God in the Ordinary
Struck Down but Not Destroyed
Sill, Silent, and Strong
Finding Hope in Hard Things
The Book of Giving
I Am a Human
The Great Lie
God of Words
Christmas Glory

Other Poetry Collections

word by Word: Prose Poems Inspired by Scripture

CONTENTS

IMAGES OF GRIEF   1

   Toby's Poem   3
   Two Loves Lost   5
   Like Water   8
   Gardener to Son   9
   My Father's Blood   10
   Love and Grief   11
   Death Came Quietly   12
   Διθάλασσον 'Between Seas'   13
   Death's Door Closed   15
   Traveler   16
   We Didn't Know   17

IMAGES FROM THE WILD WORLD   19

   Hawk   20
   Lender   21
   Isaiah 40:6   22
   Clementine   23
   A Way In   24
   March 5, 2007   25
   Wind   26
   Shaking Leaves   27
   The Lake   28
   Candle   29
   Burning the Trash   30
   Driftwood   31
   Genius   32
   The Bird   33
   Dog   34
   Egress   35
   Silence   36
   Open Field   37
   Dogs Barking   38
   The Seed   39
   Fossil   40

Cocoon   41
Braille   42
Completion   43
Fish   44
The Gardener   45

IMAGES FROM FAITH   46
God of Dust   47
From a Dream   48
Jesus's Prayer   49
Darkness   50
The Way of Words   51
John 8:17   52
Shatterer   53
Jacob   54
Your Voice   55
His Black Bible   56
Miracles   57
Genesis   58
Mark 1:9–12   59
Canine Prophet   60
Fleeting Words   61
Holiness on September 11, 2001   62

IMAGES OF GRIEF

Toby's Poem

Our father was a sturdy hull,
with his own standing sail,
but the cancer hollowed him
and the mast of his splintered mind.
On a June night,
he drifted
in a silent tempest,
on a silent sea,
to a silent country.
And that turned us all to boats.

Daily now we undock in the morning,
throwing harbor rope
to waiting water.

Daily now we stare inward at ourselves,
checking for leaks
and rusty nails.
We are boats that bob
on nervous water,
praying to the horizon,
asking the light for time,
claiming ourselves strong and free
on the wild open sea.

But none of the boats belong to us,
or their sails stitched from cotton seed,
or the oars and deck boards.
We are not owners.

We borrow.
We borrowed and planned to give back,
but then . . .

changed our minds.

Two Loves Lost

First love:
our gathering took his body
back to the cold earth,
and we prayed there
beneath a red tent.
We still pray
(But no one goes back).
Rumors of some gift lost
circulated in the hands of
expressed condolences.
We smiled,
and gave amen to weakness.

…

That summer the ocean was medicinal.
The sun was a wide knife, revealing incisions
the soul wants kept in a basement.
Soft ice was the water.
I left the pores of my body exposed to the salt
and gave the Atlantic my back,
my bones raised and offered
on the quiet altar of grief.

…

The cat was painted porcelain;
no creature ever sat so still.
His faded olive eyes

burn through my temperament
and begin the long, arduous process of analysis.
I have nothing to offer him
but the silence.
This he receives with approval
and turns to the world outside the windows.

…

The garbage burns through the trees,
rising as water up through the leaves.
My heart contracts with the rest of my life
to a piece of paper
covered with penciled words.

…

Second love:
Nana was a fine wine
we had our fill of again and again
before she returned
as a grape to the ground.

…

We never could manage the garden,
but snap peas have emerged
from the weeds by the poolside,
and the spine of a tomato plant
asks his one long question of the sun.

He will ask until his death.
Then he will sink low
so that his memory is gone
when resurrection
brings him out again,
renewed, stronger.

…

Cancer is birth.
We untangle ourselves
from the barbed wire of despair
like a bird shakes free
from string and bits of garbage.
Somewhere within us we identify
the color orange and the sunrise.

…

Gratitude finds its way:
a heavy milk beneath our bones,
lifting us up gradually,
as a wave rises with us in it.
In the distance:
Black bumps of land.

Like Water

"Like water spilled on the ground, which cannot be recovered…" (2 Samuel 14:14)

In a hospital room of white linen
and metal gates
he lay as a bowl tilted,
emptied of half of himself.
(Life absorbs as by a cloth.)

We watched his eyes intently then.
We had no container to put him in.

Weeks later he died
in a living room,
the vessel emptied,
a mirror on the wooden floor.
It has long since evaporated
and we have turned to wasps,
still seeking the place
where the water was.
So death's rag stays wet,
Allowing you to build your nest,
but the sun knows well
how to skeleton your home,
wind brushing from the window
what you call your own.

Gardener to Son

Boy, death is no un-weeded garden.
Stop pulling pieces of thought
growing in around me.
Don't turn me demigod
with the rest of the dead.
My sacredness
covers your hands;
don't let them sit idle.

The wheelbarrow is broken,
tire turned up,
leaf wrapped and heavy with boredom.
Don't be the barrow.
Let your thoughts grow, boy;
let me go here.
Wash my metal-jeweled dirt
from your peeling hands.
Let me lay under light awhile.
You go.
You go and garden.

My Father's Blood

Under the knife of a surgeon
dressed in white,
they opened the shell of his head,
taking out bits of tumor,
wiping the blood on that white,
absorbent gauze.
All over their hands,
streaked in finger marks
over stomachs and waists,
the inside screamed outside;
his inner water let free,
a stone removed from the river.
His inner water, my inner water,
his life, my life, my giver.

Love and Grief

Love grows into you.
First shell,
then fossil.
In the loss,
we would stay angry at the shell forever,
though we used to be only rock.

All the rage we had
for want of impression
evaporated with contentment.
Then love became a part of us.
We grew comfortable.
We grew hard.

Now in the absence,
we turn sandstone
and have trouble holding together
the shape we begged for.

Death Came Quietly

In the summer he slipped in the back door,
sat in the rocking chair not rocking,
sat at the dining table not dining,
stood by the fireplace not cold.
When we went to gather wood,
He followed behind us,
carrying the frozen pieces
back to the stove.

There we warmed our bones,
almost forgot he was there,
were almost truly surprised
when he left with him.

Διθάλασσον 'Between Seas'

First sea:
we played in the waves
and coughed up the salt, laughing.
The sun would not be kept out;
through the bubbled water
our hands reached down and touched silk.
We had hallelujah on our breath,
the kind you do not speak.

Sandbar:
There we walked through the waves,
spat in the sea (our skin was disturbed),
arms of iron and legs of stone.
We carried him the last several miles.
He was heavy alone.
What marrow his soul had
composed itself and stayed quiet.
There on the shore, we breathed breaths.
His last three we counted
during the night.
We awoke with the cold air,
one less.

Second sea:
We picked ourselves up,
found a boat faded from sun,

picked up the oars,
and counted ourselves.
We trusted and trust our hearts
to wood beneath us.

Death's Door Closed

It was a hard and heavy door.
I raged, I stormed, I did not conquer.
The blood and the splinters,
the swollen hands,
I used to write myself an anthem:

My country 'tis of thee,
sweet land of perjury,
of thee I'm free.

Traveler

Death made me a traveler.
My door opened:
there I huddled in the naked corner.

My door opened:
there my bones grew tight and thin.

Death made me a traveler.
I tried to send him away,
but my lips sealed as a rusty gate,
when I knew he would stay.

We Didn't Know

We came to the Cape when our bones were still soft.
And we didn't know.

The tired green waves;
the serviceberry and the crab apple trees
hugging the walkway,
Whose wooden steps led us down into silk;
The brick paths lining the town's artery;
The cedar scales of the houses;
The hyacinth and hydrangea in their purple coats;
The dune grasses and the light that combed their
hair;
Seals black as shining coal bobbing in the harbor;
Red River sand the color of blood drying;
All of these . . . resigned themselves to black and
white.

After his death,
We didn't know the colors would run—
But they didn't run together.
They went their separate ways,
Hitchhiking out of our memories.
What could we do to beckon them back?
It was too late by then.
Our bones had set in place now.
We were hard-faced, distrusting.

We didn't know
That the green waves would grey;

that the serviceberry and the crab apple trees
Rimming the beach top would sigh into charcoal;
That the wooden steps leading down to the silk
Would whiten when the oil from our feet had run dry;
That the red brick would fade to amber, then to yel-
low, then to beige,
Letting out a final breath in the white distance;
That the cedar scales would tire of breathing the sea
air
and blend blithely into the old trees;
That the hyacinth and hydrangea would shy away
from the sun
And offer up their petals to a colorless brush;
That the grasses would begin disappearing into the
white sun blade by blade;
That the seals shine would turn to matted black;
That the Red River sand would scab over and peel
away.
We didn't know.

But we keep the names of the colors
Etched on a small piece of paper in the back pocket
of our grief,
Pulling it out now and then,
Weeping, grinning, gathering,
Before stowing it away.

IMAGES FROM THE WILD WORLD

Hawk

A redtail caught in an updraft
writes out his circles for me,
steady and slow.
He's opened himself up,
hollow bones floating
in the hollows of the sky.
Only blue is at his back.

He has everything
because he has nothing.
I want his kingly poverty,
and I beg
in the deafening wind.

I would give my money,
my home,
my clothes,
to be that poor and free.

Lender

Here.
Here is
an orange.
Here is a dog.
Here are your hands; make rivers.
Here are your brothers,
and there behind you,
your mother:
blood-soil of miracles.
Here is your father,
and afterwards,
his shadow.
A borrower and a lender be.

Isaiah 40:6

The fields have enough hair now
for the hands of the wind,
thick as feathers
on the black back of a crow,
covering the nakedness of the earth.

Resilience:

they cut   rise.
        you   you
                down. Up

Some secret in the dirt
begs the sun and rain for grace.
Granted. Revoked. Granted.

Job is every blade of grass.

Clementine

Your skin
I pulled apart
and found a cold center.
I commenced halving your heart,
though I could just as easily
take the whole.

A tiny bubble climbs
the last heart section;
a lazy fish in an orange ocean
condemning my noise.
Why do I talk when I eat?

A Way In

Each of us, this is what we want:
an old book, our father's shirt,
a stone from the driveway,
a way in.

And for those moments
we leave the skin.
The soul seems to stand on a different planet.
It puts out its premature wings
through the rib cage, hints at flight,
but then returns you to the ground,
to the old book, your father's shirt,
a stone in the driveway.

March 5, 2007

The trees lay down their darker selves
on the white snow.
Next to the burn barrel
sits garbage in a towing bed,
ripe in the sun.
An old newspaper flaps in the wind,
and a plastic bag dances
next to a rusty tire.
Threads from old clothes,
as sentences, grow thin and let go,
taking their place in the wind.
All things are going.

Wind

Blustering voice,
run through me.
Move pieces of garbage
and bits of grass from my soul,
as you do in the cornfields
by the roadway.
Red Sea part my self
so I can stare on ahead
at the city I cannot dream of,
passed the water and the clouds,
with the buildings
in their block language
written on the skyline.
Here, surrounded by you,
the ink of my pen
spreads out in a river,
offering direction,
something that rises above
all this movement.

Shaking Leaves

The aspen leaves outside
are pushing their backs into the light,
knowing the days are getting shorter.
Their pride has faded
to a musty yellow at the edges.
In the gentle wind of cold November
they shudder
like my niece's back at the NICU
on the third day,
or like my grandmother's hands
at the end of her thousands.
"Come in," I say.
"Come in, leaf shaking."

The Lake

The mirror shakes its images
before returning them
to still reflection.

Nearly silent, but for the wind
In the hemlock needles.

The echo of a voice
Reaches me from the other side.
Did he say "Death" or "Yes"?

Small crumbs of stone and petrified wood,
tree bones, dribble to the edge
in the wagging body of the wind,
going under what they lorded over.

I am here happy as a heart drumming.

Candle

Bird's feet tied to wick,
thrashing and turning;
orange smile in the dark;
soldier in a field,
surrounded by wind.
Its wish:
to grow strong when it's quiet
and push its body back and forth,
learning the room
by shouldering the shadow.

Its wish:
to remain a tiny blue core
when the wind comes close;
to stay lit, hold the blue secret for the world
until it quiets down.

Its wish, like mine:
to grow up again.

Burning the Trash

I stopped burning the trash this morning,
took the gray cat
out onto the back porch
to show him the world
we keep from him.

Wind roars through the trees.
Crows caw.
The pool, covered with autumn's hands,
ripples dirty water to the edge
of the black tarp.
The smoke from the burning trash
rushes to the garden of the woods,
telling the bark words unread
from Sunday news.

The cat's eyes move like a bird's neck,
not quite able to see
everything
everywhere
at every time.

Driftwood

I brought the drift wood
from the leg of Massachusetts
to rest quietly on my night stand.
I have brushed the sand
from its tight, cracked skin.
I have dried it in the sun.
I have turned it to decoration:
a thing fit for a table.

No match for the green sea,
tide in and tide out,
under the sun, under the stars,
like a deer bone in the autumn woods.

Though we have grown akin,
like watch to wrist,
our greatest difference remains:
I am so used to carrying on;
you, so used to being carried.

Genius

I am certain my dog understands more of war,
love, discovery, joy,
and disappointment
than I could know as purely in a lifetime.
And he will live less than I will.
And he sleeps close to fourteen hours a day.
And he uses nonverbal communication
to relay his greatest needs.

What would he do, I wonder,
with words?

The Bird

The sun came up.
A crow swooped down from a silver maple,
picking up twigs, fallen hair, and grass,
leaving the rest of the world
out in the open,
as he flapped swiftly to the edge of the morning
before I lost him forever.
Life is gracious only,
Not forever and.

Dog

My bark echoes through the birches,
makes its way down the pavement,
drifts above the road grates.
This is how I un-collar myself,
how I reach for freedom.

My sound, bound to black gums
and rusted teeth,
jumps as a horse through water
and finds its freedom
in the noticing.

Egress

"You must get out."
That's what I heard from his ghost.
"The word is your handle."
That's what I learned.
Food I would cry for;
Sound I would burn for;
Light I would die for.

"You must get out,"
Is what I hear.
Utensils down, napkin folded;
like him,
I leave the whole house
an empty structure.

Silence

Silence is the shadow of the winter,
following slowly
behind the cold.

It is January,
so I wait for him.

He does not grow tired
as shadows do in the twilight,
crossing from West to East,
but is so imminently patient
for me.

Like a great beast in the zoo,
he knows I am petrified of him,
were it not for the steel bars
that keep my noise safe.

Open Field

It's surrounded
by rough trees for hair.
Old farm equipment
and cracked tires are tangled in it.
The colors on the red tractor,
wedged in the young, white birches,
are chipped and peeling like dry skin.
The tires have settled comfortably in the earth.

Corrosion is an old scar
that whispers its story
to every passing car,
a story of how, whatever it is,
it does not belong.
Though orphaned, each foreign thing is accepted
by the field.
Each settles into passive corruption.

Fields remain open as a home
to any unwanted thing,
asking no questions.
Always offering,
always receiving
as an altar.

Dogs Barking

Across the lawns I stare into the dark,
finding nothing.
My clothes feel big;
my body tired from no one thing.
What is it you want
dogs in the dark?
Red meat? Frisbee?
Old dirty tennis ball?

Would you like to trade—
to use my hands for a day
while I voice myself freely
to every stranger?

Take them.
They are used more for stealing and receiving
than for giving and forgiving.

I am the rich man,
covered in muddy rags
and the lie of innocence,
going out into the streets
with his empty metal cup,
begging for alms
from his neighbors.

The Seed

Darkness inside the seed
warms itself, as Rilke said,
"a thing just as it is."
The shell softens;
the earth around calls to it
from the outside.
All light hovers bright
as a domed universe
measured in inches.
He is patient.
Growth requires a grand disaster.

Fossil

Love is the fossil,
the hard shape
in the rock beneath you,
there without your asking.

Only when you dig it up,
notice the empty impression,
the endless hollow,
does pain emerge from detail.

Staring at your hands,
then to the ground,
wishing for life to put a shape there.

And then she offers you soft bone,
asks you to enter into stone with her,
and you happily made a hard shape
in the rock,
marking the world.

Cocoon

I suffer.
Bound by a hard shell,
hung by a branch.
I have no hands to reach,
and I burn to be burned.

Long suffering:
Calloused eyes shed a dead film.
The color green appears
as pieces of myself fall under me.
This was my worst fear.

Short suffering:
I have wings, (Did you know this?)
pasted to my back as folded paper.
Color enters me from every side.
If I do not leave, I'll burst;
if I do, I'll explode.

Braille

Braille is God's language,
the inside of the outside.
To converse you must blind yourself,
stretch out your arms
the way an infant does in sleep,
And learn the texture in the dark.
It may take a lifetime.

Completion

One more book,
another morning opened,
a list penned up and items crossed through,
completed.

Another prayer let go,
another wish realized
or melted away with time.
That last item you've discovered unnecessary,
discarded.

Sitting with hands folded,
seeing the present
with the future,
taking a breath,
just . . . believing.

Fish

We are fish too,
But our water isn't blue;
We hold our breath before death,
We gill in the old
And fin away the new.

The Gardener

Long, thin evergreen bushes
drawn out on the mulch:
this is his sanctuary;
this is his church.
The red roses he prunes
with red shears.
The Black-eyed Susans
he waters with a black bucket.
Every one of them has roots
intimate with his finger tips.

His wife has passed.

The house is quiet.
He lives only for growth now.
Photosynthesis, his priest,
Intercedes for him the with the sun,
Which rises with "A"
And falls with "men."

IMAGES FROM FAITH

God of Dust

Early afternoon in late December:
Clouds covering the face of the sun
Parted and let light flood the living room,
A current picking up carpet fibers and dog hair,
Offering them up on tiny thermals,
An ordinary sacrifice
From time to eternity.
One small dust particle dances,
Pirouettes, waltzes, sighs,
And descends, drifting back
Into the blue and white carpet.
This—that is what you tell them—
this is why I believe.

From a Dream

God makes faith
a hard stone,
casts it into a house of glass,
mapping fractures—
a ground zero thought.

Then there is no substance left
keeping you from seeing the plain colors of the sea
and that boat floating on the tired, blue water,
throwing its shoulders
left and right
on the ocean
that bears it up.

Jesus's Prayer

He goes high up
on a mountainside to pray.
Maker to maker,
nose to nose.
Wealth is buried
beneath union.

Darkness

We have been told
to push it with illumination,
cut it with candle,
ignore it with noise.

But, oh darkness,
refiner of credence,
arena of light,
house of divine dialogue,
how poorly we see you.
Darkness, name below all names,
road to revelation.

The Way of Words

Words are
as dirt and breath
and nothing less.
Rub them on your skin;
like a dog rubs his body in the dust.
Act on the scent:
A must of sound
Must turn graphic.

Let the words commune
With you and I.
We who die must find
A union to survive.

Salvation sleeps in speech.

John 8:17

The earth is parchment.
Look up from your feet,
and the sun will blind you;
stare too long and even your toes grow restless.
When the foot lifts as a wave
it carries with it dust fragments of memory.
There, behind it, an impression:
a mouth through shape
gives wings to words.

Shatterer

Decimation is a teacher.
I learn best from
seeing the pieces on the ground,
shards of building,
blades of glass,
pieces of myself.
How could they manage
to form one thing?

When I think I see,
bruise my eye, Shatterer.
Take these words
I have traced with hands;
spell them YHWH.
Bend the letter in front of me;
frustrate it.
Teach me to speak by touch.

Jacob

Hand meets neck,
skin on dirt,
God is the blessing
we know will hurt.

Back laceration,
red writing,
nails that dig and pull
as hands on a mountain.

Man and angel meet before the river,
taker and giver,
blesser and blessed,
rumbling until the sky glows gray,
giving their best.

Your Voice

There are sounds on the other side
of the dirt walls.

Punching turns sediment to stone
as I look for you, God of earth,
blowing through a clean passage
as wind whistling:
a tunnel of innocence
I cannot fit myself into.

I have tunneled the ground,
a badger looking for his God,
holding every heartbeat in a wall,
shoveling with nails
bloodied and stained with dirt—
all to get at your voice.
A trial for the hands
is a trial for the ears.

His Black Bible

Here his fingers have been—
nails tough as boat hulls,
hair sparse as swine skin,
authors of hope and hammer swing,
gloves of identity.

His hands here
went over the pages,
as feet slowly in the leaves,
moving the debris of ego
to make room for my fingers:
hands of the next season.

Miracles

I am no alien to miracles.
I make it across the field each day,
an empty bucket in hand,
oblivious to shrapnel and mortar shell,
accidentally ducking round after round,
coming back with water
through the same mess,
and having no answer
for where the well is
when I emerge from the trees.

Genesis

For "let there be,"
there was no "let there be."
Before before,
there was conversation in the dark.
Then light came loud as train,
and it became difficult
to hear the sound in the darkness,
the words that drifted as boats
from person to person to person

Mark 1:9–12

He came out dripping,
steeped in Spirit,
so much so that John could hear it:
every drip a word dropped
loud as thunder;
and his wool-soaked clothing,
heavy with resurrection,
spoke also
of a holy river.

Canine Prophet

He needs no one to tell him to roll in the dirt,
cover himself in ashes,
parade the streets
barking of the nation's impending collapse
from ignored grace.
Look at his face.
No Jeremiah stacking stones.
A step ahead of Isaiah, already happily naked.
And our unbearable silence
turns him downward at the neck,
letting his face fall, as a scribe for us.
Early in the morning he walks,
red leash swaggering on the ground
beneath the woodwind birds.
This is his kingdom.

Fleeting Words

You cannot stitch water to wood.
We tried this.
Sun un-rivets and takes back.

Our second plan was to kill the wood
And stain it with meaning,
But then fire laughed and water chuckled:
"Look at them try; look!"

Of course, to a flame or a brook
What is recording but ash or ants
Caught up in a dance?

Holiness on September 11, 2001

Holiness dissolves
as salt in water.
When we stop moving,
we see it gathered
in a sediment pile at our feet
as those at ground zero
gathered it in their hands . . .

weeping.